ONE DAY AT A TIM

MONDAY'S **MOOD**

TUESDAY'S **MOOD**

WEDNESDAY'S **MOOD**

THURSDAY'S **MOOD**

ONE DAY AT A TIME

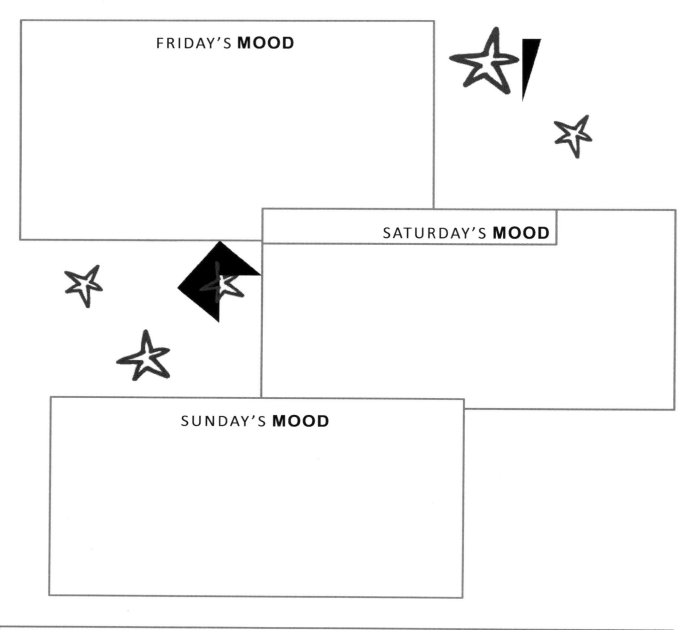

FRIDAY'S **MOOD**

SATURDAY'S **MOOD**

SUNDAY'S **MOOD**

THOUGHTS & REFLECTIONS ABOUT THE PAST WEEK

AFFIRMATIONS

DAILY AFFIRMATIONS

IDEAS & PROMPTS

I'm in charge of how I feel today, and I'm choosing to be happy.

I'm brave enough to climb any mountain.

I have the power to change my story.

I've decided that I'm good enough.

No one can make me feel inferior.

My strength is greater than my struggle.

I'll use my failures as a stepping stone.

It's not their job to like me. It's mine.

Success will be my driving force.

The only person who can defeat me, is me.

I dare to be different.

I do not need other people to be happy.

I deserve love, happiness and success.

I am loved and I am wanted.

I will not apologize for being myself.

POSITIVE THINKING

SELF CARE TO DO LIST:

- ☐ _____
- ☐ _____
- ☐ _____
- ☐ _____
- ☐ _____
- ☐ _____
- ☐ _____
- ☐ _____
- ☐ _____
- ☐ _____
- ☐ _____
- ☐ _____
- ☐ _____
- ☐ _____

PHYSICAL NEEDS

EMOTIONAL NEEDS

HOW I FEEL TODAY

I WANT TO WORK ON...

ME TIME

Write down the things that make you happy. Then, check the box every day that you spend time with that activity.

	☐ ☐ ☐ ☐ ☐ ☐ ☐
	☐ ☐ ☐ ☐ ☐ ☐ ☐
	☐ ☐ ☐ ☐ ☐ ☐ ☐
	☐ ☐ ☐ ☐ ☐ ☐ ☐
	☐ ☐ ☐ ☐ ☐ ☐ ☐
	☐ ☐ ☐ ☐ ☐ ☐ ☐
	☐ ☐ ☐ ☐ ☐ ☐ ☐
	☐ ☐ ☐ ☐ ☐ ☐ ☐

Do what makes you Happy

SELF CARE CHECKLIST

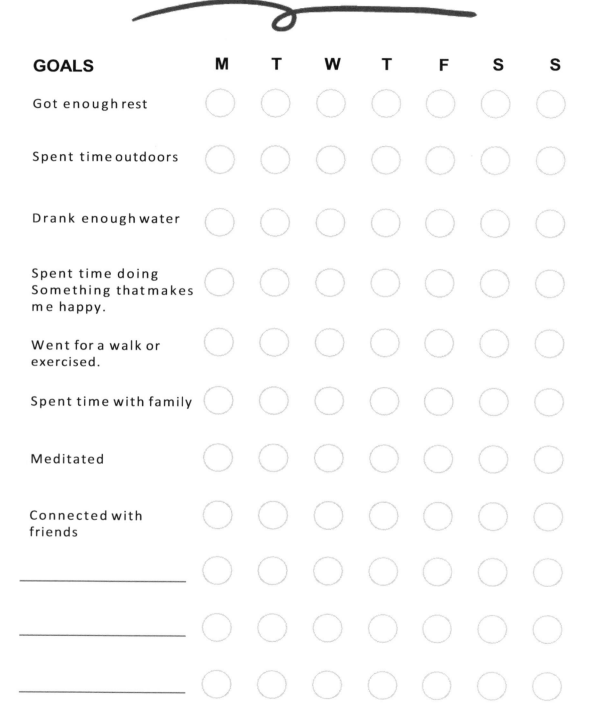

GOALS	M	T	W	T	F	S	S
Got enough rest	○	○	○	○	○	○	○
Spent time outdoors	○	○	○	○	○	○	○
Drank enough water	○	○	○	○	○	○	○
Spent time doing Something that makes me happy.	○	○	○	○	○	○	○
Went for a walk or exercised.	○	○	○	○	○	○	○
Spent time with family	○	○	○	○	○	○	○
Meditated	○	○	○	○	○	○	○
Connected with friends	○	○	○	○	○	○	○
_____	○	○	○	○	○	○	○
_____	○	○	○	○	○	○	○
_____	○	○	○	○	○	○	○

PERSONAL GOALS

MY SELF GOALS FOR THIS YEAR:

2 THINGS I CAN CHANGE TO MEET MY GOALS:

MY GREATEST OBSTACLE GOING FORWARD:

Good things take time

MENTAL HEALTH MONITOR

DAILY

_____

_____

_____

_____

_____

_____

_____

_____

_____

_____

_____

WEEKLY

_____

_____

_____

_____

_____

_____

_____

_____

_____

_____

_____

PERSONAL REFLECTIONS

SELF CARE TECHNIQUES

MIND

_____
_____
_____
_____
_____
_____
_____
_____
_____
_____
_____
_____

BODY

_____
_____
_____
_____
_____
_____
_____
_____
_____
_____
_____

SELF CARE LOG

HOW I CAN **MINIMIZE THE NEGATIVITY** IN MY LIFE

POSITIVE STEPS I CAN TAKE TO BE HAPPY

SELF CARE

DAILY INSPIRATION

WATER INTAKE:

FITNESS GOALS

One day at a time...

THANKFUL FOR

DAILY MEALS

BREAKFAST:

LUNCH:

DINNER:

SNACKS:

SELF CARE GOALS

TIME FRAME	MY GOALS	STEPS I'LL TAKE

be wild ~ be true ~ be happy

GRATEFUL THOUGHTS

THIS WEEK I AM GRATEFUL FOR

I AM BLESSED TO HAVE THESE PEOPLE IN MY LIFE

5 REASONS TO BE THANKFUL

1
2
3
4
5

POSITIVE THINKING

POSITIVE THOUGHTS:
WRITE DOWN YOUR FAVORITE INSPIRATIONAL PHRASE

Do what makes you Happy

AFFIRMATION:

ONE DAY AT A TIME

MONDAY'S **MOOD**

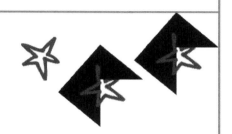

TUESDAY'S **MOOD**

WEDNESDAY'S **MOOD**

THURSDAY'S **MOOD**

ONE DAY AT A TIME

FRIDAY'S **MOOD**

SATURDAY'S **MOOD**

SUNDAY'S **MOOD**

THOUGHTS & REFLECTIONS ABOUT THE PAST WEEK

AFFIRMATIONS

DAILY AFFIRMATIONS	IDEAS & PROMPTS

IDEAS & PROMPTS

I'm in charge of how I feel today, and I'm choosing to be happy.

I'm brave enough to climb any mountain.

I have the power to change my story.

I've decided that I'm good enough.

No one can make me feel inferior.

My strength is greater than my struggle.

I'll use my failures as a stepping stone.

It's not their job to like me. It's mine.

Success will be my driving force.

The only person who can defeat me, is me.

I dare to be different.

I do not need other people to be happy.

I deserve love, happiness and success.

I am loved and I am wanted.

I will not apologize for being myself.

POSITIVE THINKING

SELF CARE TO DO LIST:

- ☐ _____
- ☐ _____
- ☐ _____
- ☐ _____
- ☐ _____
- ☐ _____
- ☐ _____
- ☐ _____
- ☐ _____
- ☐ _____
- ☐ _____
- ☐ _____
- ☐ _____
- ☐ _____

PHYSICAL NEEDS

EMOTIONAL NEEDS

HOW I FEEL TODAY

I WANT TO WORK ON...

ME TIME

Write down the things that make you happy. Then, check the box every day that you spend time with that activity.

SELF CARE CHECKLIST

GOALS	M	T	W	T	F	S	S
Got enough rest	○	○	○	○	○	○	○
Spent time outdoors	○	○	○	○	○	○	○
Drank enough water	○	○	○	○	○	○	○
Spent time doing Something that makes me happy.	○	○	○	○	○	○	○
Went for a walk or exercised.	○	○	○	○	○	○	○
Spent time with family	○	○	○	○	○	○	○
Meditated	○	○	○	○	○	○	○
Connected with friends	○	○	○	○	○	○	○
_____	○	○	○	○	○	○	○
_____	○	○	○	○	○	○	○
_____	○	○	○	○	○	○	○

PERSONAL GOALS

MY SELF GOALS FOR THIS YEAR:

2 THINGS I CAN CHANGE TO MEET MY GOALS:

MY GREATEST OBSTACLE GOING FORWARD:

Good things take time

MENTAL HEALTH MONITOR

DAILY

_____

_____

_____

_____

_____

_____

_____

_____

_____

_____

_____

WEEKLY

_____

_____

_____

_____

_____

_____

_____

_____

_____

_____

_____

PERSONAL REFLECTIONS

SELF CARE TECHNIQUES

MIND

_____

_____

_____

_____

_____

_____

_____

_____

_____

_____

_____

BODY

_____

_____

_____

_____

_____

_____

_____

_____

_____

_____

_____

SELF CARE LOG

HOW I CAN **MINIMIZE THE NEGATIVITY** IN MY LIFE

POSITIVE STEPS I CAN TAKE TO BE HAPPY

SELF CARE

DAILY **INSPIRATION**

DAILY **MEALS**

BREAKFAST:

_____

_____

_____

WATER INTAKE:

LUNCH:

_____

_____

_____

FITNESS **GOALS**

_____

_____

_____

DINNER:

_____

_____

_____

One day at a time...

SNACKS:

THANKFUL **FOR**

_____

_____

_____

_____

SELF CARE GOALS

TIME FRAME	MY GOALS	STEPS I'LL TAKE

be wild ~ be true ~ be happy

GRATEFUL THOUGHTS

THIS WEEK I AM GRATEFUL FOR

I AM BLESSED TO HAVE THESE PEOPLE IN MY LIFE

5 REASONS TO BE THANKFUL

1
2
3
4
5

POSITIVE THINKING

POSITIVE THOUGHTS:
WRITE DOWN YOUR FAVORITE INSPIRATIONAL PHRASE

Do what makes you Happy

AFFIRMATION:

ONE DAY AT A TIME

MONDAY'S **MOOD**

TUESDAY'S **MOOD**

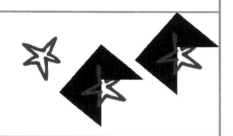

WEDNESDAY'S **MOOD**

THURSDAY'S **MOOD**

ONE DAY AT A TIME

FRIDAY'S **MOOD**

SATURDAY'S **MOOD**

SUNDAY'S **MOOD**

THOUGHTS & REFLECTIONS ABOUT THE PAST WEEK

AFFIRMATIONS

DAILY AFFIRMATIONS

IDEAS & PROMPTS

I'm in charge of how I feel today, and I'm choosing to be happy.

I'm brave enough to climb any mountain.

I have the power to change my story.

I've decided that I'm good enough.

No one can make me feel inferior.

My strength is greater than my struggle.

I'll use my failures as a stepping stone.

It's not their job to like me. It's mine.

Success will be my driving force.

The only person who can defeat me, is me.

I dare to be different.

I do not need other people to be happy.

I deserve love, happiness and success.

I am loved and I am wanted.

I will not apologize for being myself.

POSITIVE THINKING

SELF CARE TO DO LIST:

- ☐ _____
- ☐ _____
- ☐ _____
- ☐ _____
- ☐ _____
- ☐ _____
- ☐ _____
- ☐ _____
- ☐ _____
- ☐ _____
- ☐ _____
- ☐ _____
- ☐ _____
- ☐ _____

PHYSICAL NEEDS

EMOTIONAL NEEDS

HOW I FEEL TODAY

I WANT TO WORK ON...

ME TIME

Write down the things that make you happy. Then, check the box every day that you spend time with that activity.

SELF CARE CHECKLIST

GOALS	M	T	W	T	F	S	S
Got enough rest	○	○	○	○	○	○	○
Spent time outdoors	○	○	○	○	○	○	○
Drank enough water	○	○	○	○	○	○	○
Spent time doing Something that makes me happy.	○	○	○	○	○	○	○
Went for a walk or exercised.	○	○	○	○	○	○	○
Spent time with family	○	○	○	○	○	○	○
Meditated	○	○	○	○	○	○	○
Connected with friends	○	○	○	○	○	○	○
_____	○	○	○	○	○	○	○
_____	○	○	○	○	○	○	○
_____	○	○	○	○	○	○	○

PERSONAL GOALS

MY SELF GOALS FOR THIS YEAR:

2 THINGS I CAN CHANGE TO MEET MY GOALS:

MY GREATEST OBSTACLE GOING FORWARD:

Good things take time

MENTAL HEALTH MONITOR

DAILY

_____

_____

_____

_____

_____

_____

_____

_____

_____

_____

_____

WEEKLY

_____

_____

_____

_____

_____

_____

_____

_____

_____

_____

_____

PERSONAL REFLECTIONS

SELF CARE TECHNIQUES

MIND

BODY

_____

_____

_____

_____

_____

_____

_____

_____

_____

_____

_____

SELF CARE LOG

HOW I CAN **MINIMIZE THE NEGATIVITY** IN MY LIFE

POSITIVE STEPS I CAN TAKE TO BE HAPPY

SELF CARE

DAILY **INSPIRATION**

DAILY **MEALS**

BREAKFAST:

_____
_____
_____

LUNCH:

_____
_____
_____

DINNER:

_____
_____
_____

SNACKS:

_____
_____
_____
_____

WATER INTAKE:

FITNESS **GOALS**

_____
_____
_____

One day at a time...

THANKFUL **FOR**

SELF CARE GOALS

TIME FRAME	MY GOALS	STEPS I'LL TAKE

be wild ~ be true ~ be happy

GRATEFUL THOUGHTS

THIS WEEK I AM GRATEFUL FOR

I AM BLESSED TO HAVE THESE PEOPLE IN MY LIFE

5 REASONS TO BE THANKFUL

1
2
3
4
5

POSITIVE THINKING

POSITIVE THOUGHTS:
WRITE DOWN YOUR FAVORITE INSPIRATIONAL PHRASE

Do what makes you Happy

AFFIRMATION:

ONE DAY AT A TIME

MONDAY'S **MOOD**

TUESDAY'S **MOOD**

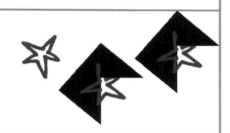

WEDNESDAY'S **MOOD**

THURSDAY'S **MOOD**

ONE DAY AT A TIME

FRIDAY'S **MOOD**

SATURDAY'S **MOOD**

SUNDAY'S **MOOD**

THOUGHTS & REFLECTIONS ABOUT THE PAST WEEK

AFFIRMATIONS

DAILY AFFIRMATIONS

IDEAS & PROMPTS

I'm in charge of how I feel today, and I'm choosing to be happy.

I'm brave enough to climb any mountain.

I have the power to change my story.

I've decided that I'm good enough.

No one can make me feel inferior.

My strength is greater than my struggle.

I'll use my failures as a stepping stone.

It's not their job to like me. It's mine.

Success will be my driving force.

The only person who can defeat me, is me.

I dare to be different.

I do not need other people to be happy.

I deserve love, happiness and success.

I am loved and I am wanted.

I will not apologize for being myself.

POSITIVE THINKING

SELF CARE TO DO LIST:

- [ ] _____
- [ ] _____
- [ ] _____
- [ ] _____
- [ ] _____
- [ ] _____
- [ ] _____
- [ ] _____
- [ ] _____
- [ ] _____
- [ ] _____
- [ ] _____
- [ ] _____

PHYSICAL NEEDS

EMOTIONAL NEEDS

HOW I FEEL TODAY

I WANT TO WORK ON...

ME TIME

Write down the things that make you happy. Then, check the box every day that you spend time with that activity.

☐	☐	☐	☐	☐	☐	☐
☐	☐	☐	☐	☐	☐	☐
☐	☐	☐	☐	☐	☐	☐
☐	☐	☐	☐	☐	☐	☐
☐	☐	☐	☐	☐	☐	☐
☐	☐	☐	☐	☐	☐	☐
☐	☐	☐	☐	☐	☐	☐
☐	☐	☐	☐	☐	☐	☐

Do what makes you Happy

SELF CARE CHECKLIST

GOALS	M	T	W	T	F	S	S
Got enough rest	◯	◯	◯	◯	◯	◯	◯
Spent time outdoors	◯	◯	◯	◯	◯	◯	◯
Drank enough water	◯	◯	◯	◯	◯	◯	◯
Spent time doing Something that makes me happy.	◯	◯	◯	◯	◯	◯	◯
Went for a walk or exercised.	◯	◯	◯	◯	◯	◯	◯
Spent time with family	◯	◯	◯	◯	◯	◯	◯
Meditated	◯	◯	◯	◯	◯	◯	◯
Connected with friends	◯	◯	◯	◯	◯	◯	◯
_____	◯	◯	◯	◯	◯	◯	◯
_____	◯	◯	◯	◯	◯	◯	◯
_____	◯	◯	◯	◯	◯	◯	◯

PERSONAL GOALS

MY SELF GOALS FOR THIS YEAR:

2 THINGS I CAN CHANGE TO MEET MY GOALS:

MY GREATEST OBSTACLE GOING FORWARD:

Good things take time

MENTAL HEALTH MONITOR

DAILY

_____

_____

_____

_____

_____

_____

_____

_____

_____

_____

_____

WEEKLY

_____

_____

_____

_____

_____

_____

_____

_____

_____

_____

_____

PERSONAL REFLECTIONS

SELF CARE TECHNIQUES

MIND

_____

_____

_____

_____

_____

_____

_____

_____

_____

_____

_____

_____

BODY

_____

_____

_____

_____

_____

_____

_____

_____

_____

_____

_____

_____

SELF CARE LOG

HOW I CAN **MINIMIZE THE NEGATIVITY** IN MY LIFE

POSITIVE STEPS I CAN TAKE TO BE HAPPY

SELF CARE

DAILY INSPIRATION

WATER INTAKE:

FITNESS GOALS

_____
_____
_____

One day at a time...

THANKFUL FOR

DAILY MEALS

BREAKFAST:

_____
_____
_____

LUNCH:

_____
_____

DINNER:

_____
_____

SNACKS:

_____
_____
_____
_____

SELF CARE GOALS

TIME FRAME	MY GOALS	STEPS I'LL TAKE

be wild ~ be true ~ be happy

GRATEFUL THOUGHTS

THIS WEEK I AM GRATEFUL FOR

I AM BLESSED TO HAVE THESE PEOPLE IN MY LIFE

5 REASONS TO BE THANKFUL

1
2
3
4
5

POSITIVE THINKING

POSITIVE THOUGHTS:
WRITE DOWN YOUR FAVORITE INSPIRATIONAL PHRASE

Do what makes you Happy

AFFIRMATION:

ONE DAY AT A TIME

MONDAY'S **MOOD**

TUESDAY'S **MOOD**

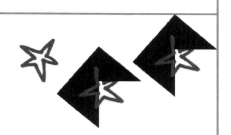

WEDNESDAY'S **MOOD**

THURSDAY'S **MOOD**

ONE DAY AT A TIME

FRIDAY'S **MOOD**

SATURDAY'S **MOOD**

SUNDAY'S **MOOD**

THOUGHTS & REFLECTIONS ABOUT THE PAST WEEK

AFFIRMATIONS

DAILY AFFIRMATIONS

IDEAS & PROMPTS

I'm in charge of how I feel today, and I'm choosing to be happy.

I'm brave enough to climb any mountain.

I have the power to change my story.

I've decided that I'm good enough.

No one can make me feel inferior.

My strength is greater than my struggle.

I'll use my failures as a stepping stone.

It's not their job to like me. It's mine.

Success will be my driving force.

The only person who can defeat me, is me.

I dare to be different.

I do not need other people to be happy.

I deserve love, happiness and success.

I am loved and I am wanted.

I will not apologize for being myself.

POSITIVE THINKING

SELF CARE TO DO LIST:

- ☐ _____
- ☐ _____
- ☐ _____
- ☐ _____
- ☐ _____
- ☐ _____
- ☐ _____
- ☐ _____
- ☐ _____
- ☐ _____
- ☐ _____
- ☐ _____
- ☐ _____
- ☐ _____

PHYSICAL NEEDS

EMOTIONAL NEEDS

HOW I FEEL TODAY

I WANT TO WORK ON...

ME TIME

Write down the things that make you happy. Then, check the box every day that you spend time with that activity.

	☐ ☐ ☐ ☐ ☐ ☐ ☐
	☐ ☐ ☐ ☐ ☐ ☐ ☐
	☐ ☐ ☐ ☐ ☐ ☐ ☐
	☐ ☐ ☐ ☐ ☐ ☐ ☐
	☐ ☐ ☐ ☐ ☐ ☐ ☐
	☐ ☐ ☐ ☐ ☐ ☐ ☐
	☐ ☐ ☐ ☐ ☐ ☐ ☐
	☐ ☐ ☐ ☐ ☐ ☐ ☐

Do what makes you Happy

SELF CARE CHECKLIST

GOALS	M	T	W	T	F	S	S
Got enough rest	○	○	○	○	○	○	○
Spent time outdoors	○	○	○	○	○	○	○
Drank enough water	○	○	○	○	○	○	○
Spent time doing Something that makes me happy.	○	○	○	○	○	○	○
Went for a walk or exercised.	○	○	○	○	○	○	○
Spent time with family	○	○	○	○	○	○	○
Meditated	○	○	○	○	○	○	○
Connected with friends	○	○	○	○	○	○	○
_____	○	○	○	○	○	○	○
_____	○	○	○	○	○	○	○
_____	○	○	○	○	○	○	○

PERSONAL GOALS

MY SELF GOALS FOR THIS YEAR:

2 THINGS I CAN CHANGE TO MEET MY GOALS:

MY GREATEST OBSTACLE GOING FORWARD:

Good things take time

MENTAL HEALTH MONITOR

DAILY

_____

_____

_____

_____

_____

_____

_____

_____

_____

_____

_____

WEEKLY

_____

_____

_____

_____

_____

_____

_____

_____

_____

_____

_____

PERSONAL REFLECTIONS

SELF CARE TECHNIQUES

MIND

_____

_____

_____

_____

_____

_____

_____

_____

_____

_____

_____

BODY

_____

_____

_____

_____

_____

_____

_____

_____

_____

_____

_____

SELF CARE LOG

HOW I CAN **MINIMIZE THE NEGATIVITY** IN MY LIFE

POSITIVE STEPS I CAN TAKE TO BE HAPPY

SELF CARE

DAILY **INSPIRATION**

WATER INTAKE:

FITNESS **GOALS**

_____
_____
_____

One day at a time...

THANKFUL **FOR**

DAILY **MEALS**

BREAKFAST:

_____
_____
_____

LUNCH:

_____
_____

DINNER:

_____
_____

SNACKS:

_____
_____
_____

SELF CARE GOALS

TIME FRAME	MY GOALS	STEPS I'LL TAKE

be wild ~ be true ~ be happy

GRATEFUL THOUGHTS

THIS WEEK I AM GRATEFUL FOR

I AM BLESSED TO HAVE THESE PEOPLE IN MY LIFE

5 REASONS TO BE THANKFUL

1
2
3
4
5

POSITIVE THINKING

POSITIVE THOUGHTS:
WRITE DOWN YOUR FAVORITE INSPIRATIONAL PHRASE

Do what makes you Happy

AFFIRMATION:

ONE DAY AT A TIME

MONDAY'S **MOOD**

TUESDAY'S **MOOD**

WEDNESDAY'S **MOOD**

THURSDAY'S **MOOD**

ONE DAY AT A TIME

FRIDAY'S **MOOD**

SATURDAY'S **MOOD**

SUNDAY'S **MOOD**

THOUGHTS & REFLECTIONS ABOUT THE PAST WEEK

AFFIRMATIONS

DAILY AFFIRMATIONS

IDEAS & PROMPTS

I'm in charge of how I feel today, and I'm choosing to be happy.

I'm brave enough to climb any mountain.

I have the power to change my story.

I've decided that I'm good enough.

No one can make me feel inferior.

My strength is greater than my struggle.

I'll use my failures as a stepping stone.

It's not their job to like me. It's mine.

Success will be my driving force.

The only person who can defeat me, is me.

I dare to be different.

I do not need other people to be happy.

I deserve love, happiness and success.

I am loved and I am wanted.

I will not apologize for being myself.

POSITIVE THINKING

SELF CARE TO DO LIST:

- [ ] _____
- [ ] _____
- [ ] _____
- [ ] _____
- [ ] _____
- [ ] _____
- [ ] _____
- [ ] _____
- [ ] _____
- [ ] _____
- [ ] _____
- [ ] _____
- [ ] _____
- [ ] _____

PHYSICAL NEEDS

EMOTIONAL NEEDS

HOW I FEEL TODAY

I WANT TO WORK ON...

ME TIME

Write down the things that make you happy. Then, check the box every day that you spend time with that activity.

	☐	☐	☐	☐	☐	☐	☐
	☐	☐	☐	☐	☐	☐	☐
	☐	☐	☐	☐	☐	☐	☐
	☐	☐	☐	☐	☐	☐	☐
	☐	☐	☐	☐	☐	☐	☐
	☐	☐	☐	☐	☐	☐	☐
	☐	☐	☐	☐	☐	☐	☐
	☐	☐	☐	☐	☐	☐	☐

Do what makes you Happy

SELF CARE CHECKLIST

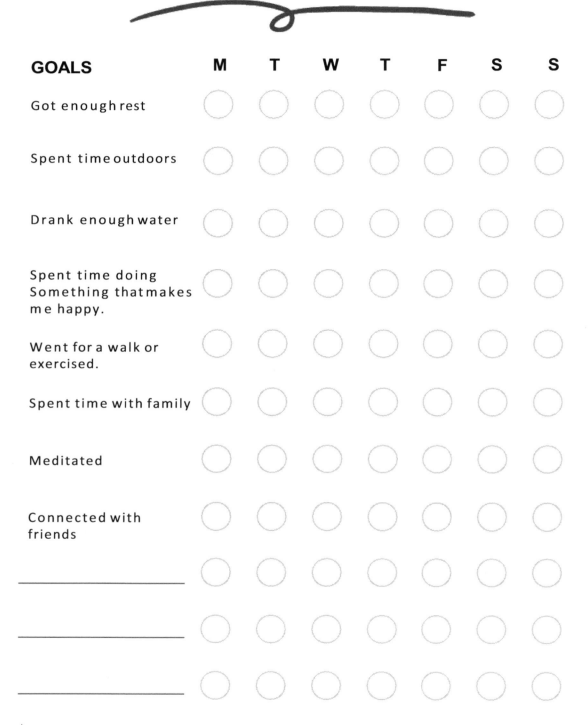

GOALS	M	T	W	T	F	S	S
Got enough rest	○	○	○	○	○	○	○
Spent time outdoors	○	○	○	○	○	○	○
Drank enough water	○	○	○	○	○	○	○
Spent time doing Something that makes me happy.	○	○	○	○	○	○	○
Went for a walk or exercised.	○	○	○	○	○	○	○
Spent time with family	○	○	○	○	○	○	○
Meditated	○	○	○	○	○	○	○
Connected with friends	○	○	○	○	○	○	○
_____	○	○	○	○	○	○	○
_____	○	○	○	○	○	○	○
_____	○	○	○	○	○	○	○

PERSONAL GOALS

MY SELF GOALS FOR THIS YEAR:

2 THINGS I CAN CHANGE TO MEET MY GOALS:

MY GREATEST OBSTACLE GOING FORWARD:

Good things take time

MENTAL HEALTH MONITOR

DAILY

_____
_____
_____
_____
_____
_____
_____
_____
_____
_____
_____

WEEKLY

_____
_____
_____
_____
_____
_____
_____
_____
_____

PERSONAL REFLECTIONS

SELF CARE TECHNIQUES

MIND

_____
_____
_____
_____
_____
_____
_____
_____
_____
_____
_____
_____

BODY

_____
_____
_____
_____
_____
_____
_____
_____
_____
_____
_____
_____

SELF CARE LOG

HOW I CAN **MINIMIZE THE NEGATIVITY** IN MY LIFE

POSITIVE STEPS I CAN TAKE TO BE HAPPY

SELF CARE

DAILY **INSPIRATION**

DAILY **MEALS**

BREAKFAST:

_____

_____

_____

WATER INTAKE:

LUNCH:

_____

_____

_____

FITNESS **GOALS**

_____

_____

_____

DINNER:

_____

_____

_____

One day at a time...

SNACKS:

THANKFUL **FOR**

_____

_____

_____

_____

_____

SELF CARE GOALS

TIME FRAME	MY GOALS	STEPS I'LL TAKE

be wild ~ be true ~ be happy

GRATEFUL THOUGHTS

THIS WEEK I AM GRATEFUL FOR

I AM BLESSED TO HAVE THESE PEOPLE IN MY LIFE

5 REASONS TO BE THANKFUL

1
2
3
4
5

POSITIVE THINKING

POSITIVE THOUGHTS:
WRITE DOWN YOUR FAVORITE INSPIRATIONAL PHRASE

Do what makes you Happy

AFFIRMATION:

ONE DAY AT A TIME

MONDAY'S **MOOD**

TUESDAY'S **MOOD**

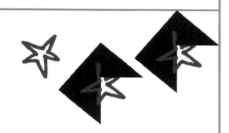

WEDNESDAY'S **MOOD**

THURSDAY'S **MOOD**

ONE DAY AT A TIME

FRIDAY'S **MOOD**

SATURDAY'S **MOOD**

SUNDAY'S **MOOD**

THOUGHTS & REFLECTIONS ABOUT THE PAST WEEK

AFFIRMATIONS

DAILY AFFIRMATIONS

IDEAS & PROMPTS

I'm in charge of how I feel today, and I'm choosing to be happy.

I'm brave enough to climb any mountain.

I have the power to change my story.

I've decided that I'm good enough.

No one can make me feel inferior.

My strength is greater than my struggle.

I'll use my failures as a stepping stone.

It's not their job to like me. It's mine.

Success will be my driving force.

The only person who can defeat me, is me.

I dare to be different.

I do not need other people to be happy.

I deserve love, happiness and success.

I am loved and I am wanted.

I will not apologize for being myself.

POSITIVE THINKING

SELF CARE TO DO LIST:

- ☐ _____
- ☐ _____
- ☐ _____
- ☐ _____
- ☐ _____
- ☐ _____
- ☐ _____
- ☐ _____
- ☐ _____
- ☐ _____
- ☐ _____
- ☐ _____
- ☐ _____
- ☐ _____

PHYSICAL NEEDS

EMOTIONAL NEEDS

HOW I FEEL TODAY

I WANT TO WORK ON...

ME TIME

Write down the things that make you happy. Then, check the box every day that you spend time with that activity.

	☐	☐	☐	☐	☐	☐	☐
	☐	☐	☐	☐	☐	☐	☐
	☐	☐	☐	☐	☐	☐	☐
	☐	☐	☐	☐	☐	☐	☐
	☐	☐	☐	☐	☐	☐	☐
	☐	☐	☐	☐	☐	☐	☐
	☐	☐	☐	☐	☐	☐	☐
	☐	☐	☐	☐	☐	☐	☐

Do what makes you Happy

SELF CARE CHECKLIST

GOALS	M	T	W	T	F	S	S
Got enough rest	○	○	○	○	○	○	○
Spent time outdoors	○	○	○	○	○	○	○
Drank enough water	○	○	○	○	○	○	○
Spent time doing Something that makes me happy.	○	○	○	○	○	○	○
Went for a walk or exercised.	○	○	○	○	○	○	○
Spent time with family	○	○	○	○	○	○	○
Meditated	○	○	○	○	○	○	○
Connected with friends	○	○	○	○	○	○	○
_____	○	○	○	○	○	○	○
_____	○	○	○	○	○	○	○
_____	○	○	○	○	○	○	○

PERSONAL GOALS

MY SELF GOALS FOR THIS YEAR:

2 THINGS I CAN CHANGE TO MEET MY GOALS:

MY GREATEST OBSTACLE GOING FORWARD:

Good things take time

MENTAL HEALTH MONITOR

DAILY

_____

_____

_____

_____

_____

_____

_____

_____

_____

_____

WEEKLY

_____

_____

_____

_____

_____

_____

_____

_____

_____

_____

PERSONAL REFLECTIONS

SELF CARE TECHNIQUES

MIND

_____
_____
_____
_____
_____
_____
_____
_____
_____
_____
_____

BODY

_____
_____
_____
_____
_____
_____
_____
_____
_____
_____
_____

SELF CARE LOG

HOW I CAN **MINIMIZE THE NEGATIVITY** IN MY LIFE

POSITIVE STEPS I CAN TAKE TO BE HAPPY

SELF CARE

DAILY **INSPIRATION**

WATER INTAKE:

FITNESS **GOALS**

One day at a time...

THANKFUL **FOR**

DAILY **MEALS**

BREAKFAST:

LUNCH:

DINNER:

SNACKS:

SELF CARE GOALS

TIME FRAME	MY GOALS	STEPS I'LL TAKE

be wild ～ be true ～ be happy

GRATEFUL THOUGHTS

THIS WEEK I AM GRATEFUL FOR

I AM BLESSED TO HAVE THESE PEOPLE IN MY LIFE

5 REASONS TO BE THANKFUL

1
2
3
4
5

POSITIVE THINKING

POSITIVE THOUGHTS:
WRITE DOWN YOUR FAVORITE INSPIRATIONAL PHRASE

Do what makes you Happy

AFFIRMATION:

ONE DAY AT A TIME

MONDAY'S **MOOD**

TUESDAY'S **MOOD**

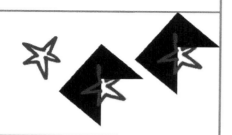

WEDNESDAY'S **MOOD**

THURSDAY'S **MOOD**

ONE DAY AT A TIME

FRIDAY'S **MOOD**

SATURDAY'S **MOOD**

SUNDAY'S **MOOD**

THOUGHTS & REFLECTIONS ABOUT THE PAST WEEK

AFFIRMATIONS

DAILY AFFIRMATIONS

IDEAS & PROMPTS

I'm in charge of how I feel today, and I'm choosing to be happy.

I'm brave enough to climb any mountain.

I have the power to change my story.

I've decided that I'm good enough.

No one can make me feel inferior.

My strength is greater than my struggle.

I'll use my failures as a stepping stone.

It's not their job to like me. It's mine.

Success will be my driving force.

The only person who can defeat me, is me.

I dare to be different.

I do not need other people to be happy.

I deserve love, happiness and success.

I am loved and I am wanted.

I will not apologize for being myself.

POSITIVE THINKING

SELF CARE TO DO LIST:

- ☐ _____
- ☐ _____
- ☐ _____
- ☐ _____
- ☐ _____
- ☐ _____
- ☐ _____
- ☐ _____
- ☐ _____
- ☐ _____
- ☐ _____
- ☐ _____
- ☐ _____
- ☐ _____

PHYSICAL NEEDS

EMOTIONAL NEEDS

HOW I FEEL TODAY

I WANT TO WORK ON...

ME TIME

Write down the things that make you happy. Then, check the box every day that you spend time with that activity.

	☐	☐	☐	☐	☐	☐	☐
	☐	☐	☐	☐	☐	☐	☐
	☐	☐	☐	☐	☐	☐	☐
	☐	☐	☐	☐	☐	☐	☐
	☐	☐	☐	☐	☐	☐	☐
	☐	☐	☐	☐	☐	☐	☐
	☐	☐	☐	☐	☐	☐	☐
	☐	☐	☐	☐	☐	☐	☐

Do what makes you Happy

SELF CARE CHECKLIST

GOALS	M	T	W	T	F	S	S
Got enough rest	○	○	○	○	○	○	○
Spent time outdoors	○	○	○	○	○	○	○
Drank enough water	○	○	○	○	○	○	○
Spent time doing Something that makes me happy.	○	○	○	○	○	○	○
Went for a walk or exercised.	○	○	○	○	○	○	○
Spent time with family	○	○	○	○	○	○	○
Meditated	○	○	○	○	○	○	○
Connected with friends	○	○	○	○	○	○	○
_____	○	○	○	○	○	○	○
_____	○	○	○	○	○	○	○
_____	○	○	○	○	○	○	○

PERSONAL GOALS

MY SELF GOALS FOR THIS YEAR:

2 THINGS I CAN CHANGE TO MEET MY GOALS:

MY GREATEST OBSTACLE GOING FORWARD:

Good things take time

MENTAL HEALTH MONITOR

DAILY

_____

_____

_____

_____

_____

_____

_____

_____

_____

_____

WEEKLY

_____

_____

_____

_____

_____

_____

_____

_____

_____

_____

PERSONAL REFLECTIONS

SELF CARE TECHNIQUES

MIND

_____
_____
_____
_____
_____
_____
_____
_____
_____
_____
_____

BODY

_____
_____
_____
_____
_____
_____
_____
_____
_____
_____

SELF CARE LOG

HOW I CAN **MINIMIZE THE NEGATIVITY** IN MY LIFE

POSITIVE STEPS I CAN TAKE TO BE HAPPY

SELF CARE

DAILY **INSPIRATION**

WATER INTAKE:

FITNESS **GOALS**

One day at a time...

THANKFUL **FOR**

DAILY **MEALS**

BREAKFAST:

_____
_____
_____

LUNCH:

_____
_____
_____

DINNER:

_____
_____
_____

SNACKS:

_____
_____
_____

SELF CARE GOALS

TIME FRAME	MY GOALS	STEPS I'LL TAKE

be wild ∼∘∼ *be true* ∼∘∼ *be happy*

GRATEFUL THOUGHTS

THIS WEEK I AM GRATEFUL FOR

I AM BLESSED TO HAVE THESE PEOPLE IN MY LIFE

5 REASONS TO BE THANKFUL

1
2
3
4
5

POSITIVE THINKING

POSITIVE THOUGHTS:
WRITE DOWN YOUR FAVORITE INSPIRATIONAL PHRASE

Do what makes you Happy

AFFIRMATION:

ONE DAY AT A TIME

MONDAY'S **MOOD**

TUESDAY'S **MOOD**

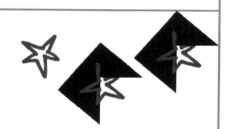

WEDNESDAY'S **MOOD**

THURSDAY'S **MOOD**

ONE DAY AT A TIME

FRIDAY'S **MOOD**

SATURDAY'S **MOOD**

SUNDAY'S **MOOD**

THOUGHTS & REFLECTIONS ABOUT THE PAST WEEK

AFFIRMATIONS

DAILY AFFIRMATIONS

IDEAS & PROMPTS

I'm in charge of how I feel today, and I'm choosing to be happy.

I'm brave enough to climb any mountain.

I have the power to change my story.

I've decided that I'm good enough.

No one can make me feel inferior.

My strength is greater than my struggle.

I'll use my failures as a stepping stone.

It's not their job to like me. It's mine.

Success will be my driving force.

The only person who can defeat me, is me.

I dare to be different.

I do not need other people to be happy.

I deserve love, happiness and success.

I am loved and I am wanted.

I will not apologize for being myself.

POSITIVE THINKING

SELF CARE TO DO LIST:

☐ _____

☐ _____

☐ _____

☐ _____

☐ _____

☐ _____

☐ _____

☐ _____

☐ _____

☐ _____

☐ _____

☐ _____

☐ _____

☐ _____

PHYSICAL NEEDS

EMOTIONAL NEEDS

HOW I FEEL TODAY

I WANT TO WORK ON...

ME TIME

Write down the things that make you happy. Then, check the box every day that you spend time with that activity.

☐	☐	☐	☐	☐	☐	☐
☐	☐	☐	☐	☐	☐	☐
☐	☐	☐	☐	☐	☐	☐
☐	☐	☐	☐	☐	☐	☐
☐	☐	☐	☐	☐	☐	☐
☐	☐	☐	☐	☐	☐	☐
☐	☐	☐	☐	☐	☐	☐
☐	☐	☐	☐	☐	☐	☐

Do what makes you Happy

SELF CARE CHECKLIST

GOALS	M	T	W	T	F	S	S
Got enough rest	○	○	○	○	○	○	○
Spent time outdoors	○	○	○	○	○	○	○
Drank enough water	○	○	○	○	○	○	○
Spent time doing Something that makes me happy.	○	○	○	○	○	○	○
Went for a walk or exercised.	○	○	○	○	○	○	○
Spent time with family	○	○	○	○	○	○	○
Meditated	○	○	○	○	○	○	○
Connected with friends	○	○	○	○	○	○	○
_____	○	○	○	○	○	○	○
_____	○	○	○	○	○	○	○
_____	○	○	○	○	○	○	○

PERSONAL GOALS

MY SELF GOALS FOR THIS YEAR:

2 THINGS I CAN CHANGE TO MEET MY GOALS:

MY GREATEST OBSTACLE GOING FORWARD:

Good things take time

MENTAL HEALTH MONITOR

DAILY

_____

_____

_____

_____

_____

_____

_____

_____

_____

_____

WEEKLY

_____

_____

_____

_____

_____

_____

_____

_____

_____

_____

PERSONAL REFLECTIONS

SELF CARE TECHNIQUES

MIND

BODY

_____

_____

_____

_____

_____

_____

_____

_____

_____

_____

_____

SELF CARE LOG

HOW I CAN **MINIMIZE THE NEGATIVITY** IN MY LIFE

POSITIVE STEPS I CAN TAKE TO BE HAPPY

SELF CARE

DAILY INSPIRATION

DAILY MEALS

BREAKFAST:

_____

_____

_____

LUNCH:

_____

_____

_____

WATER INTAKE:

DINNER:

_____

FITNESS GOALS

_____

_____

_____

_____

SNACKS:

_____

One day at a time...

THANKFUL FOR

_____

_____

_____

SELF CARE GOALS

TIME FRAME	MY GOALS	STEPS I'LL TAKE

be wild ~ be true ~ be happy

GRATEFUL THOUGHTS

THIS WEEK I AM GRATEFUL FOR

I AM BLESSED TO HAVE THESE PEOPLE IN MY LIFE

5 REASONS TO BE THANKFUL

1
2
3
4
5

POSITIVE THINKING

POSITIVE THOUGHTS:
WRITE DOWN YOUR FAVORITE INSPIRATIONAL PHRASE

Do what makes you Happy

AFFIRMATION:

ONE DAY AT A TIME

MONDAY'S **MOOD**

TUESDAY'S **MOOD**

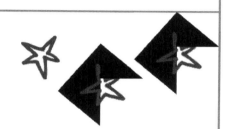

WEDNESDAY'S **MOOD**

THURSDAY'S **MOOD**

ONE DAY AT A TIME

FRIDAY'S **MOOD**

SATURDAY'S **MOOD**

SUNDAY'S **MOOD**

THOUGHTS & REFLECTIONS ABOUT THE PAST WEEK

AFFIRMATIONS

DAILY AFFIRMATIONS

IDEAS & PROMPTS

I'm in charge of how I feel today, and I'm choosing to be happy.

I'm brave enough to climb any mountain.

I have the power to change my story.

I've decided that I'm good enough.

No one can make me feel inferior.

My strength is greater than my struggle.

I'll use my failures as a stepping stone.

It's not their job to like me. It's mine.

Success will be my driving force.

The only person who can defeat me, is me.

I dare to be different.

I do not need other people to be happy.

I deserve love, happiness and success.

I am loved and I am wanted.

I will not apologize for being myself.

POSITIVE THINKING

SELF CARE TO DO LIST:

- ☐ _____
- ☐ _____
- ☐ _____
- ☐ _____
- ☐ _____
- ☐ _____
- ☐ _____
- ☐ _____
- ☐ _____
- ☐ _____
- ☐ _____
- ☐ _____
- ☐ _____
- ☐ _____

PHYSICAL NEEDS

EMOTIONAL NEEDS

HOW I FEEL TODAY

I WANT TO WORK ON...

ME TIME

Write down the things that make you happy. Then, check the box every day that you spend time with that activity.

	☐	☐	☐	☐	☐	☐	☐
	☐	☐	☐	☐	☐	☐	☐
	☐	☐	☐	☐	☐	☐	☐
	☐	☐	☐	☐	☐	☐	☐
	☐	☐	☐	☐	☐	☐	☐
	☐	☐	☐	☐	☐	☐	☐
	☐	☐	☐	☐	☐	☐	☐
	☐	☐	☐	☐	☐	☐	☐

Do what makes you Happy

SELF CARE CHECKLIST

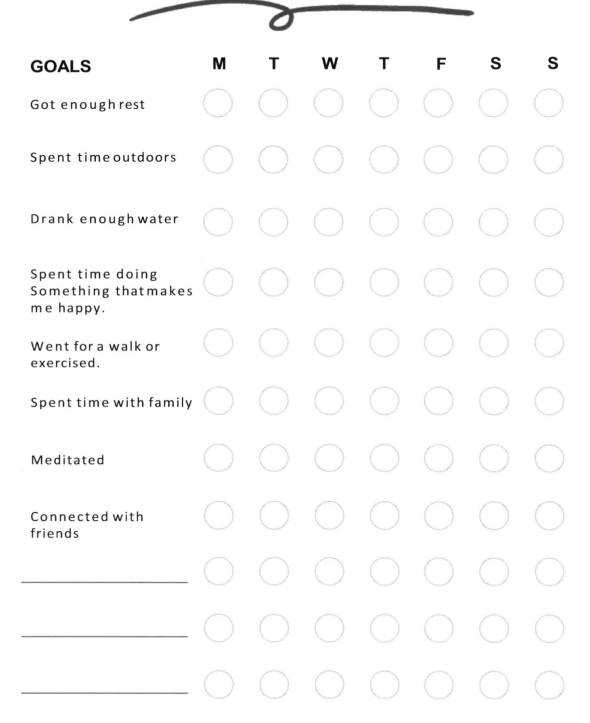

GOALS	M	T	W	T	F	S	S
Got enough rest	◯	◯	◯	◯	◯	◯	◯
Spent time outdoors	◯	◯	◯	◯	◯	◯	◯
Drank enough water	◯	◯	◯	◯	◯	◯	◯
Spent time doing Something that makes me happy.	◯	◯	◯	◯	◯	◯	◯
Went for a walk or exercised.	◯	◯	◯	◯	◯	◯	◯
Spent time with family	◯	◯	◯	◯	◯	◯	◯
Meditated	◯	◯	◯	◯	◯	◯	◯
Connected with friends	◯	◯	◯	◯	◯	◯	◯
_____	◯	◯	◯	◯	◯	◯	◯
_____	◯	◯	◯	◯	◯	◯	◯
_____	◯	◯	◯	◯	◯	◯	◯

PERSONAL GOALS

MY SELF GOALS FOR THIS YEAR:

2 THINGS I CAN CHANGE TO MEET MY GOALS:

MY GREATEST OBSTACLE GOING FORWARD:

Good things take time

MENTAL HEALTH MONITOR

DAILY

_____

_____

_____

_____

_____

_____

_____

_____

_____

_____

_____

WEEKLY

_____

_____

_____

_____

_____

_____

_____

_____

_____

_____

_____

PERSONAL REFLECTIONS

SELF CARE TECHNIQUES

MIND

_____

_____

_____

_____

_____

_____

_____

_____

_____

_____

_____

_____

BODY

_____

_____

_____

_____

_____

_____

_____

_____

_____

_____

_____

SELF CARE LOG

HOW I CAN **MINIMIZE THE NEGATIVITY** IN MY LIFE

POSITIVE STEPS I CAN TAKE TO BE HAPPY

SELF CARE

DAILY **INSPIRATION**

WATER INTAKE:

FITNESS **GOALS**

One day at a time...

THANKFUL **FOR**

DAILY **MEALS**

BREAKFAST:

_____
_____
_____

LUNCH:

_____
_____
_____

DINNER:

_____
_____
_____

SNACKS:

_____
_____
_____
_____

SELF CARE GOALS

TIME FRAME	MY GOALS	STEPS I'LL TAKE

be wild ~ *be true* ~ *be happy*

GRATEFUL THOUGHTS

THIS WEEK I AM GRATEFUL FOR

I AM BLESSED TO HAVE THESE PEOPLE IN MY LIFE

5 REASONS TO BE THANKFUL

1
2
3
4
5

POSITIVE THINKING

POSITIVE THOUGHTS:
WRITE DOWN YOUR FAVORITE INSPIRATIONAL PHRASE

Do what makes you Happy

AFFIRMATION:

ONE DAY AT A TIME

MONDAY'S **MOOD**

TUESDAY'S **MOOD**

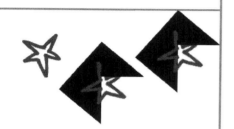

WEDNESDAY'S **MOOD**

THURSDAY'S **MOOD**

ONE DAY AT A TIME

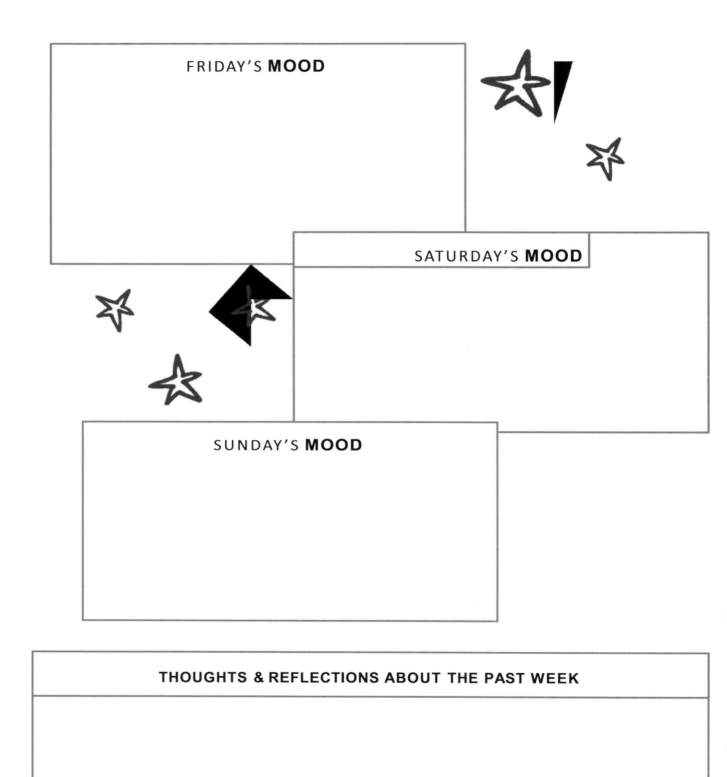

FRIDAY'S **MOOD**

SATURDAY'S **MOOD**

SUNDAY'S **MOOD**

THOUGHTS & REFLECTIONS ABOUT THE PAST WEEK

AFFIRMATIONS

DAILY AFFIRMATIONS

IDEAS & PROMPTS

I'm in charge of how I feel today, and I'm choosing to be happy.

I'm brave enough to climb any mountain.

I have the power to change my story.

I've decided that I'm good enough.

No one can make me feel inferior.

My strength is greater than my struggle.

I'll use my failures as a stepping stone.

It's not their job to like me. It's mine.

Success will be my driving force.

The only person who can defeat me, is me.

I dare to be different.

I do not need other people to be happy.

I deserve love, happiness and success.

I am loved and I am wanted.

I will not apologize for being myself.

POSITIVE THINKING

SELF CARE TO DO LIST:

- ☐ _____
- ☐ _____
- ☐ _____
- ☐ _____
- ☐ _____
- ☐ _____
- ☐ _____
- ☐ _____
- ☐ _____
- ☐ _____
- ☐ _____
- ☐ _____
- ☐ _____
- ☐ _____

PHYSICAL NEEDS

EMOTIONAL NEEDS

HOW I FEEL TODAY

I WANT TO WORK ON...

ME TIME

Write down the things that make you happy. Then, check the box every day that you spend time with that activity.

Do what makes you Happy

SELF CARE CHECKLIST

GOALS	M	T	W	T	F	S	S
Got enough rest	○	○	○	○	○	○	○
Spent time outdoors	○	○	○	○	○	○	○
Drank enough water	○	○	○	○	○	○	○
Spent time doing Something that makes me happy.	○	○	○	○	○	○	○
Went for a walk or exercised.	○	○	○	○	○	○	○
Spent time with family	○	○	○	○	○	○	○
Meditated	○	○	○	○	○	○	○
Connected with friends	○	○	○	○	○	○	○
_____	○	○	○	○	○	○	○
_____	○	○	○	○	○	○	○
_____	○	○	○	○	○	○	○

PERSONAL GOALS

MY SELF GOALS FOR THIS YEAR:

2 THINGS I CAN CHANGE TO MEET MY GOALS:

MY GREATEST OBSTACLE GOING FORWARD:

Good things take time

MENTAL HEALTH MONITOR

DAILY

_____

_____

_____

_____

_____

_____

_____

_____

_____

_____

_____

WEEKLY

_____

_____

_____

_____

_____

_____

_____

_____

_____

_____

_____

PERSONAL REFLECTIONS

SELF CARE TECHNIQUES

MIND

_____
_____
_____
_____
_____
_____
_____
_____
_____
_____
_____

BODY

_____
_____
_____
_____
_____
_____
_____
_____
_____
_____
_____

SELF CARE LOG

HOW I CAN **MINIMIZE THE NEGATIVITY** IN MY LIFE

POSITIVE STEPS I CAN TAKE TO BE HAPPY

SELF CARE

DAILY INSPIRATION

WATER INTAKE:

FITNESS GOALS

One day at a time...

THANKFUL FOR

DAILY MEALS

BREAKFAST:

_____

_____

_____

LUNCH:

_____

_____

_____

DINNER:

_____

_____

_____

SNACKS:

_____

_____

_____

_____

SELF CARE GOALS

TIME FRAME	MY GOALS	STEPS I'LL TAKE

be wild ~ be true ~ be happy

GRATEFUL THOUGHTS

THIS WEEK I AM GRATEFUL FOR

_____
_____
_____
_____
_____

I AM BLESSED TO HAVE THESE PEOPLE IN MY LIFE

_____
_____
_____
_____
_____

5 REASONS TO BE THANKFUL

1 _____
2 _____
3 _____
4 _____
5 _____

POSITIVE THINKING

POSITIVE THOUGHTS:
WRITE DOWN YOUR FAVORITE INSPIRATIONAL PHRASE

Do what makes you Happy

AFFIRMATION:

ONE DAY AT A TIME

MONDAY'S **MOOD**

TUESDAY'S **MOOD**

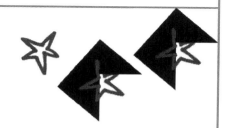

WEDNESDAY'S **MOOD**

THURSDAY'S **MOOD**

ONE DAY AT A TIME

FRIDAY'S **MOOD**

SATURDAY'S **MOOD**

SUNDAY'S **MOOD**

THOUGHTS & REFLECTIONS ABOUT THE PAST WEEK

AFFIRMATIONS

DAILY AFFIRMATIONS

IDEAS & PROMPTS

I'm in charge of how I feel today, and I'm choosing to be happy.

I'm brave enough to climb any mountain.

I have the power to change my story.

I've decided that I'm good enough.

No one can make me feel inferior.

My strength is greater than my struggle.

I'll use my failures as a stepping stone.

It's not their job to like me. It's mine.

Success will be my driving force.

The only person who can defeat me, is me.

I dare to be different.

I do not need other people to be happy.

I deserve love, happiness and success.

I am loved and I am wanted.

I will not apologize for being myself.

POSITIVE THINKING

SELF CARE TO DO LIST:

- ☐ _____
- ☐ _____
- ☐ _____
- ☐ _____
- ☐ _____
- ☐ _____
- ☐ _____
- ☐ _____
- ☐ _____
- ☐ _____
- ☐ _____
- ☐ _____
- ☐ _____
- ☐ _____

PHYSICAL NEEDS

EMOTIONAL NEEDS

HOW I FEEL TODAY

I WANT TO WORK ON...

ME TIME

Write down the things that make you happy. Then, check the box every day that you spend time with that activity.

	☐	☐	☐	☐	☐	☐	☐
	☐	☐	☐	☐	☐	☐	☐
	☐	☐	☐	☐	☐	☐	☐
	☐	☐	☐	☐	☐	☐	☐
	☐	☐	☐	☐	☐	☐	☐
	☐	☐	☐	☐	☐	☐	☐
	☐	☐	☐	☐	☐	☐	☐
	☐	☐	☐	☐	☐	☐	☐

Do what makes you Happy

SELF CARE CHECKLIST

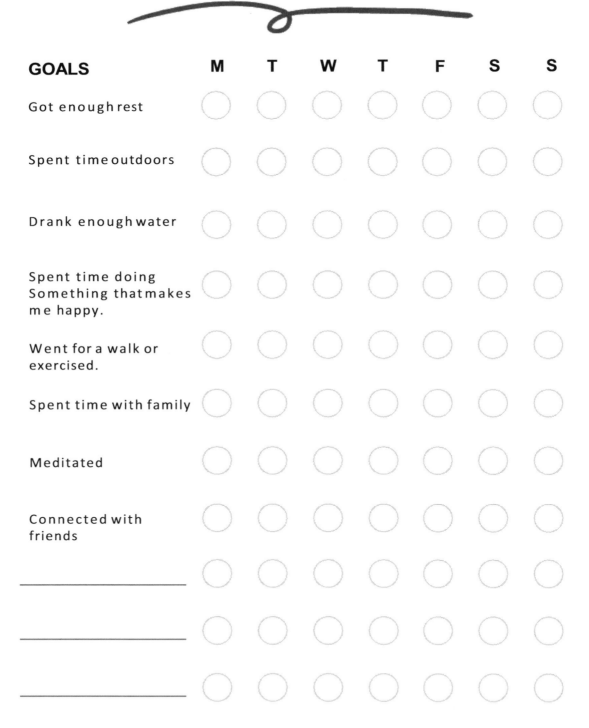

GOALS	M	T	W	T	F	S	S
Got enough rest	○	○	○	○	○	○	○
Spent time outdoors	○	○	○	○	○	○	○
Drank enough water	○	○	○	○	○	○	○
Spent time doing Something that makes me happy.	○	○	○	○	○	○	○
Went for a walk or exercised.	○	○	○	○	○	○	○
Spent time with family	○	○	○	○	○	○	○
Meditated	○	○	○	○	○	○	○
Connected with friends	○	○	○	○	○	○	○
_____	○	○	○	○	○	○	○
_____	○	○	○	○	○	○	○
_____	○	○	○	○	○	○	○

PERSONAL GOALS

MY SELF GOALS FOR THIS YEAR:

2 THINGS I CAN CHANGE TO MEET MY GOALS:

MY GREATEST OBSTACLE GOING FORWARD:

Good things take time

MENTAL HEALTH MONITOR

DAILY

_____

_____

_____

_____

_____

_____

_____

_____

_____

_____

_____

WEEKLY

_____

_____

_____

_____

_____

_____

_____

_____

_____

_____

_____

PERSONAL REFLECTIONS

SELF CARE TECHNIQUES

MIND

_____
_____
_____
_____
_____
_____
_____
_____
_____
_____
_____

BODY

_____
_____
_____
_____
_____
_____
_____
_____
_____
_____

SELF CARE LOG

HOW I CAN **MINIMIZE THE NEGATIVITY** IN MY LIFE

POSITIVE STEPS I CAN TAKE TO BE HAPPY

SELF CARE

DAILY **INSPIRATION**

WATER INTAKE:

FITNESS **GOALS**

One day at a time...

THANKFUL **FOR**

DAILY **MEALS**

BREAKFAST:

LUNCH:

DINNER:

SNACKS:

SELF CARE GOALS

TIME FRAME	MY GOALS	STEPS I'LL TAKE

be wild ~ be true ~ be happy

GRATEFUL THOUGHTS

THIS WEEK I AM GRATEFUL FOR

I AM BLESSED TO HAVE THESE PEOPLE IN MY LIFE

5 REASONS TO BE THANKFUL

1
2
3
4
5

POSITIVE THINKING

POSITIVE THOUGHTS:
WRITE DOWN YOUR FAVORITE INSPIRATIONAL PHRASE

Do what makes you Happy

AFFIRMATION:

ONE DAY AT A TIME

MONDAY'S **MOOD**

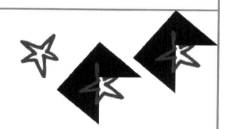

TUESDAY'S **MOOD**

WEDNESDAY'S **MOOD**

THURSDAY'S **MOOD**

ONE DAY AT A TIME

FRIDAY'S **MOOD**

SATURDAY'S **MOOD**

SUNDAY'S **MOOD**

THOUGHTS & REFLECTIONS ABOUT THE PAST WEEK

AFFIRMATIONS

DAILY AFFIRMATIONS

IDEAS & PROMPTS

I'm in charge of how I feel today, and I'm choosing to be happy.

I'm brave enough to climb any mountain.

I have the power to change my story.

I've decided that I'm good enough.

No one can make me feel inferior.

My strength is greater than my struggle.

I'll use my failures as a stepping stone.

It's not their job to like me. It's mine.

Success will be my driving force.

The only person who can defeat me, is me.

I dare to be different.

I do not need other people to be happy.

I deserve love, happiness and success.

I am loved and I am wanted.

I will not apologize for being myself.

POSITIVE THINKING

SELF CARE TO DO LIST:

- [ ] _____
- [ ] _____
- [ ] _____
- [ ] _____
- [ ] _____
- [ ] _____
- [ ] _____
- [ ] _____
- [ ] _____
- [ ] _____
- [ ] _____
- [ ] _____
- [ ] _____
- [ ] _____

PHYSICAL NEEDS

EMOTIONAL NEEDS

HOW I FEEL TODAY

I WANT TO WORK ON...

ME TIME

Write down the things that make you happy. Then, check the box every day that you spend time with that activity.

	☐	☐	☐	☐	☐	☐	☐
	☐	☐	☐	☐	☐	☐	☐
	☐	☐	☐	☐	☐	☐	☐
	☐	☐	☐	☐	☐	☐	☐
	☐	☐	☐	☐	☐	☐	☐
	☐	☐	☐	☐	☐	☐	☐
	☐	☐	☐	☐	☐	☐	☐
	☐	☐	☐	☐	☐	☐	☐

Do what makes you Happy

SELF CARE CHECKLIST

GOALS	M	T	W	T	F	S	S
Got enough rest	○	○	○	○	○	○	○
Spent time outdoors	○	○	○	○	○	○	○
Drank enough water	○	○	○	○	○	○	○
Spent time doing Something that makes me happy.	○	○	○	○	○	○	○
Went for a walk or exercised.	○	○	○	○	○	○	○
Spent time with family	○	○	○	○	○	○	○
Meditated	○	○	○	○	○	○	○
Connected with friends	○	○	○	○	○	○	○
_____	○	○	○	○	○	○	○
_____	○	○	○	○	○	○	○
_____	○	○	○	○	○	○	○

PERSONAL GOALS

MY SELF GOALS FOR THIS YEAR:

2 THINGS I CAN CHANGE TO MEET MY GOALS:

MY GREATEST OBSTACLE GOING FORWARD:

Good things take time

MENTAL HEALTH MONITOR

DAILY

_____

_____

_____

_____

_____

_____

_____

_____

_____

_____

_____

WEEKLY

_____

_____

_____

_____

_____

_____

_____

_____

_____

_____

PERSONAL REFLECTIONS

SELF CARE TECHNIQUES

MIND

_____
_____
_____
_____
_____
_____
_____
_____
_____
_____
_____
_____

BODY

_____
_____
_____
_____
_____
_____
_____
_____
_____
_____
_____

SELF CARE LOG

HOW I CAN **MINIMIZE THE NEGATIVITY** IN MY LIFE

POSITIVE STEPS I CAN TAKE TO BE HAPPY

SELF CARE

DAILY **INSPIRATION**

WATER INTAKE:

FITNESS **GOALS**

One day at a time...

THANKFUL **FOR**

DAILY **MEALS**

BREAKFAST:

_____

_____

_____

LUNCH:

_____

_____

_____

DINNER:

_____

_____

_____

SNACKS:

_____

_____

_____

_____

SELF CARE GOALS

TIME FRAME	MY GOALS	STEPS I'LL TAKE

be wild ~ be true ~ be happy

GRATEFUL THOUGHTS

THIS WEEK I AM GRATEFUL FOR

I AM BLESSED TO HAVE THESE PEOPLE IN MY LIFE

5 REASONS TO BE THANKFUL

1
2
3
4
5

POSITIVE THINKING

POSITIVE THOUGHTS:
WRITE DOWN YOUR FAVORITE INSPIRATIONAL PHRASE

Do what makes you Happy

AFFIRMATION:

ONE DAY AT A TIME

MONTH: …………..

1	2	3	4
5	6	7	8
9	10	11	12
13	14	15	16
17	18	19	20
21	22	23	24
25	26	27	28
29	30	31	

ONE DAY AT A TIME

MONTH: ……………

1	2	3	4
5	6	7	8
9	10	11	12
13	14	15	16
17	18	19	20
21	22	23	24
25	26	27	28
29	30	31	

ONE DAY AT A TIME

MONTH: …………..

1	2	3	4
5	6	7	8
9	10	11	12
13	14	15	16
17	18	19	20
21	22	23	24
25	26	27	28
29	30	31	

ONE DAY AT A TIME

MONTH: ....

1	2	3	4
5	6	7	8
9	10	11	12
13	14	15	16
17	18	19	20
21	22	23	24
25	26	27	28
29	30	31	

ONE DAY AT A TIME

MONTH: ....

1	2	3	4
5	6	7	8
9	10	11	12
13	14	15	16
17	18	19	20
21	22	23	24
25	26	27	28
29	30	31	

ONE DAY AT A TIME

MONTH: ....

1	2	3	4
5	6	7	8
9	10	11	12
13	14	15	16
17	18	19	20
21	22	23	24
25	26	27	28
29	30	31	

ONE DAY AT A TIME

MONTH: …………..

1	2	3	4
5	6	7	8
9	10	11	12
13	14	15	16
17	18	19	20
21	22	23	24
25	26	27	28
29	30	31	

ONE DAY AT A TIME

MONTH: ....

1	2	3	4
5	6	7	8
9	10	11	12
13	14	15	16
17	18	19	20
21	22	23	24
25	26	27	28
29	30	31	

ONE DAY AT A TIME

MONTH: …………..

1	2	3	4
5	6	7	8
9	10	11	12
13	14	15	16
17	18	19	20
21	22	23	24
25	26	27	28
29	30	31	

ONE DAY AT A TIME

MONTH: ....

1	2	3	4
5	6	7	8
9	10	11	12
13	14	15	16
17	18	19	20
21	22	23	24
25	26	27	28
29	30	31	

ONE DAY AT A TIME

MONTH: …………..

1	2	3	4
5	6	7	8
9	10	11	12
13	14	15	16
17	18	19	20
21	22	23	24
25	26	27	28
29	30	31	

ONE DAY AT A TIME

MONTH: ....

1	2	3	4
5	6	7	8
9	10	11	12
13	14	15	16
17	18	19	20
21	22	23	24
25	26	27	28
29	30	31	

A Year in Color

	J	F	M	A	M	J	J	A	S	O	N	D

IRRITATED, FRUSTRATED, OR ANGRY

NERVOUS, STRESSED OR ANXIOUS

ENERGIZED OR EXCITED

CALM OR RELAXED

DEPRESSED, SAD OR EMOTIONAL

ACTIVE, FOCUSED OR MOTIVATED

HAPPY, POSITIVE OR OPTIMISTIC

TIRED, RESTLESS OR UNEASY

1
2
3
4
5
6
7
8
9
10
11
12
13
14
15
16
17
18
19
20
21
22
23
24
25
26
27
28
29
30
31

Printed in Great Britain
by Amazon